BLOOMSBURY
IN 50

BUILDINGS

LUCY McMURDO

AMBERLEY

For Mac, for his constant support and without whom this book could not be written

First published 2019

Amberley Publishing, The Hill, Stroud
Gloucestershire GL5 4EP

www.amberley-books.com

Copyright © Lucy McMurdo, 2019

The right of Lucy McMurdo to be identified as the Author of this work has been asserted in accordance with the Copyrights, Designs and Patents Act 1988.

Map contains Ordnance Survey data © Crown copyright and database right [2019]

British Library Cataloguing in Publication Data.
A catalogue record for this book is available from the British Library.

ISBN 978 1 4456 5914 5 (print)
ISBN 978 1 4456 5915 2 (ebook)

Typesetting by Aura Technology and Software Services, India.
Printed in Great Britain.

Contents

Map   4

Key   5

Introduction   6

The 50 Buildings   8

Acknowledgements   96

About the Author   96

Key

1. Inns of Court
2. Red Lion Square and Conway Hall
3. Persephone Books
4. St George the Martyr Church
5. Church of St George, Bloomsbury
6. The Queen's Larder
7. Bedford Square
8. Horse Hospital
9. Sir John Soane's Museum
10. Charles Dickens Museum
11. Eastman Dental Institute
12. Heal's
13. St Pancras Church
14. Gordon Square
15. Woburn Walk
16. British Museum
17. Wilkins Building, University College London (UCL)
18. Great Ormond Street Hospital for Children (GOSH)
19. Church of Christ the King
20. James Smith & Sons
21. The Princess Louise
22. Cabmen's Shelter
23. National Hospital for Neurology and Neurosurgery
24. Peabody Buildings
25. Dairy Supply Company Ltd
26. Former Russell Hotel
27. University College London Hospital (UCLH)
28. Mary Ward House
29. The Lady Ottoline
30. The Italian Hospital
31. Imagination
32. Euston Fire Station
33. Royal Academy of Dramatic Art (RADA)
34. Russell Square Underground Station
35. Sicilian Avenue
36. Grant Museum of Zoology
37. Waterstones
38. Willing House
39. BMA House
40. Rosewood London Hotel
41. Senate House
42. Dominion Theatre
43. Former Daimler Car Hire Garage
44. The Wellcome Collection
45. Coram and the Foundling Museum
46. Congress House
47. Lumen United Reformed Church
48. The Brunswick
49. Institute of Education (IOE)
50. UCL School of Slavonic and East European Studies (SSEES)

How to Use This Book

In accordance with the *50 Buildings* series, the buildings appear in chronological order according to the time of their original construction.

Please note that the map identifies each building by a number that corresponds to the numbers used in the text.

Introduction

Packed full of academic, legal, cultural and medical institutions, as well as being graced with elegant Georgian terraces and leafy open spaces, Bloomsbury is certainly one of central London's most attractive districts. Located between London's West End and the Square Mile, it boasts the world-acclaimed British Museum and is full of fascinating history and buildings. It was the area where in the fourteenth century lawyers established their Inns of Court, yet real urban development began in earnest from the 1700s, when land owned by the Duke of Bedford was transformed from open fields into a planned grid of residential housing and garden squares. With the housing came churches, public houses and shops, and later medical and educational institutions too. During the 1900s this was where Charles Dickens lived and his one surviving house, in Doughty Street, is now a dedicated museum.

Throughout Bloomsbury's history artists and writers have been attracted to the district; the Pre-Raphaelite Brotherhood of Artists was founded here in 1848 and Bedford Square has always been a hub for professionals, especially writers, educationalists, publishers, physicians, and architects. In the early twentieth century Bloomsbury became synonymous with a bohemian circle of intellectuals known as the Bloomsbury Group (including Virginia Woolf, John Maynard Keynes, Vanessa Bell and Lytton Strachey), and English Heritage blue plaques still adorn the walls of their homes here.

Bloomsbury owes much of its character to its Georgian architecture; beautiful squares surrounded by large terraced town houses with landscaped central gardens. As different architects were involved in their development, each has its own distinct style, but this is where you will see excellent work of Samuel Pepys Cockerell, James Burton, and Thomas and Lewis Cubitt. Development has continued ever since with exciting examples of Tudor, neoclassic, Arts and Crafts, Edwardian baroque, art deco, brutalist and post-modernist architecture. Many famous architects, including Hawksmoor, Smirke, Holden, Lasdun and Hodgkinson, have contributed to its dramatic street scene.

Over the years many buildings in Bloomsbury have received English Heritage recognition for their historic and architectural interest. This 'listed status' (Grades I, II* and II) means that building work has to be approved in advance and conform to planning regulations, thus ensuring that essential features are protected, not damaged or lost. The list of such buildings is wide-ranging and includes churches, pubs, university buildings, museums and even hospitals.

Medical institutions in particular are abundant here including the world-renowned pioneering Great Ormond Street Hospital for Children (GOSH), University College Hospital London and the Wellcome Trust. Bloomsbury has always been a leader in welfare and social progress and the work of philanthropists such as Thomas Coram and George Peabody is still evident in its streets.

Today it is a remarkably vibrant, thriving area full of students and visitors. Its boundaries are not distinct but for the purposes of this book extend from Euston Road in the north to Lincoln's Inn in the south, and between Tottenham Court Road in the west and Gray's Inn Road in the east.

The 50 Buildings

1. Inns of Court: Lincoln's Inn and Gray's Inn, South Square

Located in the south-east of Bloomsbury, Lincoln's and Gray's Inns are two of the four present-day bastions of the legal profession, the Inns of Court. Here, for the past 700 years trainee lawyers have both studied and lived in a campus environment sharing facilities including a dining hall, chapel, library, chambers (originally accommodation, now mainly barristers' offices), and spacious landscaped gardens. Despite their similarities the Inns are marked by differences: Lincoln's Inn is characterised by its red-brick Gothic, Tudor-style buildings and recognised by its badge, a lion and golden millrinds; while Gray's Inn is predominantly Georgian in style with brick and stone flat-fronted buildings, and displays a gold griffin on a black field as its badge. Both Inns are loved by movie-makers on account of their historic and atmospheric locations; no wonder then that they provide

Lincoln's Inn. (© A. McMurdo)

Right: Lincoln's Inn. (© A. McMurdo)

Below: Gray's Inn Hall. (© A. McMurdo)

The Walks, Gray's Inn. (© A. McMurdo)

the backdrop to many films, TV and period dramas. In 2017 *The Children Act*, starring Emma Thompson, was interestingly filmed at both locations.

The Inns' magnificent halls have always been used for dining, and for lectures, debates, and entertainment too. In fact, it was at Gray's Inn in 1565 that William Shakespeare's *Comedy of Errors* was first performed. The Inn was also where a young Charles Dickens worked as a junior clerk in 1827 at the age of fifteen.

Gray's and Lincoln's Inns today provide pupillage, the final part of training, to trainee barristers before they ultimately qualify and are admitted to the Bar. As fully-fledged barristers they then act for clients as advocates in the courts, having first been briefed by their clients' solicitors. Cherie Blair, the human rights lawyer and wife of ex-Prime Minister Tony Blair, worked in chambers at Gray's Inn until 2014. Notable famous alumni here include Thomas Cromwell, Henry VIII's chief advisor, and Sir Francis Bacon, the celebrated statesman and Lord Chancellor. Similarly, Lincoln's Inn is associated with William Penn, founder of Pennsylvania, Baroness Margaret Thatcher and Tony Blair. For further details about the Inns see www.graysinn.org.uk and www.lincolnsinn.org.uk.

2. Red Lion Square and Conway Hall

This is one of Bloomsbury's oldest squares tucked neatly between Theobald's Road and High Holborn. When plans for its construction were revealed they caused an almighty furore. The seventeenth-century developer Nicholas Barbon was well known for his lack of scruples, a man intent on making money who was happy to pursue his schemes whatever the cost. The lawyers at nearby Gray's Inn greatly feared the proposed development, believing it would spoil the district's tranquil character and rural views. Their frustration ultimately led to a pitched battle with Barbon's workmen, but even this didn't prevent the work from going ahead. By 1684 the square, named after the popular local Red Lion Inn, was completed but today little remains of the early square apart from its layout and a row of eighteenth-century houses on its south side.

A number of famous people were once residents here including the artists Dante Gabriel Rossetti, Edward Burne-Jones and William Morris, as well as marine chronometer inventor John Harrison. The square is even said to have its own ghosts, thought to be spectres of the parliamentarian regicides Cromwell, Ireton and Bradshaw. According to legend it is their bodies lying beneath the central gardens that periodically haunt the square.

At No. 25 is Conway Hall, erected in 1929 and noted for its Arts and Crafts and art deco features. It is the headquarters of the South Place Ethical Society, named after its early leader, Moncure Daniel Conway, an American anti-slavery campaigner and committed advocate of free thought. The society, in pursuance of his beliefs, has always welcomed those who are happy to speak their mind. Nowadays, Conway Hall acts both as a hub for local community groups and as a venue for lectures, conferences, classes and musical concerts. Its impressive library is globally renowned as a major humanist research resource.

Conway Hall, Red Lion Square.
(© A. McMurdo)

In keeping with the sentiments of the society, a bust of the philosopher Bertrand Russell and a statue of Fenner Brockway, the twentieth-century anti-war activist and politician, are sited within the square.

3. Persephone Books, Lamb's Conduit Street

Persephone Books is an independent publishing house that has its own particular and decidedly individual style. The enterprise was founded just over twenty years ago by Cambridge graduate and author Nicola Beauman, in a room above a pub. She was eager to publish books, including diaries, fiction, poetry and cookbooks, from the interwar years that appealed to her, especially those with a good theme or passion, that she felt had been neglected or were no longer in print. Many, but not all of the books she was interested in were written by women and this has largely been the company's ethos ever since. So, Beauman's choice of the name, Persephone, for her business is apt as Persephone is the symbol of female creativity and of new beginnings.

Initially, the business was run from a basement in Clerkenwell but with the overnight success of Persephone book No. 21, *Miss Pettigrew Lives for a Day* by Winifred Watson (and its subsequent film adaptation), the decision was taken to move into larger premises in Lamb's Conduit Street and to open a shop there.

Today, there are more than 130 titles in the range and each is promoted by Persephone as guaranteeing a 'good read'. This has always been Nicola Beauman's guiding principle and she continues to publish only the books she totally loves.

Persephone Books.
(© A. McMurdo)

Persephone Books. (© A. McMurdo)

Some are indeed eccentric and not to everyone's taste, but Persephone refuses to cater to populist fashion, continuing its founder's original vision.

Persephone Books are easy to identify on account of their stylish silver-grey covers, patterned end papers and matching bookmarks and throughout the shop you see neatly stacked, elegant grey books lining the many bookshelves and on table displays. Concise information about the individual titles is displayed on the shelves and in greater detail in Persephone's catalogue, available in the shop or at www.persephonebooks.co.uk.

Although a small business, Persephone Books has found its niche in the market and continues Bloomsbury's enduring association with good literature and the publishing industry.

4. St George the Martyr Church, Queen Square

Walk into the building today and you may be surprised to see that it is both an Anglican church and home to a thriving coffee house extending right into the church nave. The unusual café is a magnet for local residents, visitors and students in the area.

The church originally began life as a chapel of ease (a satellite church, providing services for congregants unable to easily attend the parish church) to St Andrew's Holborn, a decade before Queen Square was developed. By the early 1720s the parish had grown to such an extent that the chapel became a parish church in its own right and was named St George the Martyr, differentiating it from

St George the Martyr Church. (© A. McMurdo)

St George's, Bloomsbury. In recent years it has changed its name to 'St George's Holborn', and today runs a lively community programme.

In the nineteenth century the church became known as the 'Sweeps' Church' when a local philanthropist, Captain James South, gave £1,000 to provide climbing boys with an annual Christmas dinner. These boys, often as young as seven or eight, were employed by chimney sweeps to clamber up inside the chimneys and remove the soot from the flues. The boys needed to be very small and were sometimes orphans or street urchins. It was their job to climb to the top of the stack from the fireplace often through labyrinthine, awkward constricted passages. It was dangerous work; they might get stuck in a narrow flue and die of suffocation or perhaps fall, breaking a leg or injuring their spine. The long-term effects of breathing in the noxious fumes meant that many of them suffered severe health problems while others died from the dreaded 'chimney sweep cancer'. Despite legislation being enacted throughout the mid-nineteenth century the practice of employing climbing boys continued until 1875 when the Chimney Sweepers Act was finally passed. At last no child under twenty-one years of age could be forced up a chimney.

Today visitors to the church can see two wall plaques remembering these times and the contribution made by Captain South.

5. Church of St George, Bloomsbury Way

The church is most famously known for its highly unusual and striking steeple, a stepped pyramid topped with a statue of George I in Roman attire. It was the handiwork of Nicholas Hawksmoor, former protégé of Sir Christopher Wren. Completed in 1730, it was one of twelve churches to be constructed under the 1711 Fifty New Churches Act at a time when London's population was rapidly expanding. Hawksmoor based the tower on one of the Seven Wonders of the Ancient World, the Mausoleum of Halicarnassus, fragments of which can still be seen today in the nearby British Museum. It was always a controversial structure and was ridiculed by many (the writer Horace Walpole called it 'a masterpiece of absurdity') as shown in a popular rhyme of the time:

> When Henry VIII left the Pope in the lurch
> The Protestants made him head of the Church
> But George's good subjects, the Bloomsbury people
> Instead of the Church, made him head of the steeple.

Throughout its lifetime St George's has been connected to many artists and writers: William Hogarth's engraving 'Gin Lane' (1751) depicts the church spire in its squalid street scene, while the church is seen in Dickens's *Sketches by Boz* as the setting of 'The Bloomsbury Christening'.

Above and right: Church spire, St George's, Bloomsbury.
(© A. McMurdo)

Interior of St George's, Bloomsbury. (© A. McMurdo)

In 1815 the author Anthony Trollope was baptised in the church, and Emily Davison, the suffragette who flung herself in front of the king's horse at the 1913 Derby, was commemorated here in a memorial service. Later, huge numbers of suffragettes accompanied her coffin through the streets to King's Cross railway station before it began its journey to the north of England.

Today, after a major restoration project one can visit Hawksmoor's wonderfully refurbished church and marvel at his use of baroque and classical architectural styles. The church crypt is now home to the Museum of Comedy, which offers an interesting and varied programme. In addition to church services St George's hosts many concerts and works tirelessly for the homeless offering them food and shelter.

6. The Queen's Larder

Queen Square

Looking across Queen Square, this attractive watering hole has been supplying food and ale for more than 300 years. The pub was built a little before the square was formed when the area was just open field. Within no time the fields had disappeared and handsome residential housing appeared on three of the square's sides. The fourth side, facing north, remained untouched so that the residents could benefit from country air and had a view of the hills of Hampstead and Highgate, adding to their general well-being and the reputation of the square.

George III became king in 1760 and reigned until 1820. He was the longest-serving British monarch until Queen Victoria, and more recently Elizabeth II, but his reign was marred by bouts of mental illness. Little was known in this period about such illnesses and treatment for the condition by today's standards was very primitive. The king's first brief episode occurred early in his reign but the next attack in 1788 was much worse and lasted longer. At this time he stayed in Queen Square in the house of his physician, Dr Willis, who was treating him. While lodging there his devoted wife, Queen Charlotte, is said to have rented space in the cellar beneath the pub to store some of the king's favourite foods. As a result of this story the pub has been known as The Queen's Larder ever since!

Throughout the king's long reign he suffered from the same illness and then recovered. His symptoms, apart from the acute mania, included blue urine and incoherency so he was thought to be suffering from porphyria, a physical genetic blood disorder. Only in recent times has it been suggested that he suffered instead from a psychiatric malady, bipolar disorder. Interestingly, Queen Square today is greatly associated with health and although several hospitals have replaced the former housing, The Queen's Larder still provides visitors with a good selection of food and drink and a warm welcome in its cosy, wood-panelled interior.

The Queen's Larder. (© A. McMurdo)

7. Bedford Square

WC1

Used as a backdrop in many movie and TV productions, Bedford Square is a superb architectural example of a complete Georgian square. It is remarkably well preserved and displays all the features of grand town houses of the period. Developed as a gated and exclusive square between 1775 and 1780 by the Bedford Estate, the elegant brick terraces are constructed around a private key garden. The town houses are arranged over five floors and display characteristic Georgian features: iron railings, intricate fanlights, mansard roofs, balconies and imposing windows. They are particularly celebrated for their doorways possessing ornate keystones with sculpted bearded faces.

The terraces were erected as quality housing and immediately attracted residents who were politicians and statesmen, lawyers, surgeons, novelists, publishers, architects and even an aristocratic society hostess (q.v. The Lady Ottoline). In time, the residential housing was replaced by business premises and today the great majority of the buildings are used as office space, many of them awarded Grade I listed status, reflecting the social and historic character of the square and its prestigious location.

Below left and right: Bedford Square. (© A. McMurdo)

Bedford Square. (© A. McMurdo)

A green plaque outside No. 48, now premises of the renowned antiquarian booksellers Maggs, states that 'Bedford College for Women University of London was founded here in 1849 by Elizabeth Jesser Reid'. The college has since become part of Royal Holloway, University of London, based in Surrey. When Mrs Reid (1789–1866) first set up her non-sectarian Ladies College it was considered most progressive yet within only thirty years women were permitted to sit exams at the University of London, and subsequently were able to pursue careers not available to them in the past.

Not only associated with higher education, the square also has strong links with the architectural profession. The eight buildings occupying Nos 32–39 are home to the Architectural Association, a major private school of architecture. Many famous British architects are alumni including Richard Rogers, Michael Hopkins, Zaha Hadid, Denys Lasdun, Nicholas Grimshaw and Quinlan Terry. Bedford Square's occupants have always reflected the nature of the area in particular its literary, intellectual and academic character.

8. Horse Hospital

Colonnade, WC1

This unique building takes us back several hundred years to a time when Bloomsbury's streets were full of horses. Until the age of modern transport, working horses were the mainstay of travel by coach and carriage and so it was

The Horse Hospital.
(© A. McMurdo)

necessary to keep the animals healthy, nourished and stabled. Purpose-built as an infirmary for sick horses, the Horse Hospital was constructed in the late 1790s, although the present building is believed to date to the Victorian era. Built on two floors with space for twenty-four horses, the hospital still retains some of its original features such as ramps, tethering rings and cast-iron pillars.

Nowadays the building is largely associated with the media and it displays artworks in the Chamber of Pop Culture, runs regular exhibitions and shows cult films in its ground-floor cinema club. The Horse Hospital advertises itself as an independent, alternative and underground arts venue specializing in everything that is non-conformist and experimental. It certainly appears to live up to its promise.

In total contrast, the upper floor houses Roger K. Burton's vintage clothes collection 'The Contemporary Wardrobe Collection', which is used by celebrities and the movie, fashion and TV industries. See www.thehorsehospital.com for more details.

9. Sir John Soane's Museum

12-14 Lincoln's Inn Fields

Sir John Soane's Museum is a truly amazing Aladdin's cave of historic antiquities, sculptures, paintings and other bizarre mementos. Nestled between terraced Georgian town houses, the museum extends across three houses, originally the family home and offices of the architect and avid art collector John Soane (1753–1837), who lived here from 1794 until his death.

Soane came from a modest background, the son of a bricklayer. At the age of fifteen he began working first for the prominent architect George Dance the Younger, then moved to the architectural offices of Henry Holland, from whom he gained excellent instruction in architectural practices. Full of ambition he attended lectures at the Royal Academy of Arts, ultimately making a name for himself.

Above left: Interior of Sir John Soane's Museum. (© Gareth Gardner)

Above right: Statue of the Ephesian Diana. (© Gareth Gardner)

This led to commissions at the Bank of England, Houses of Parliament, Westminster Law Courts as well as in many aristocratic homes. Soane's travels overseas to Italy and France in the late 1770s inspired his love of the ancient world and had a profound influence on his own architectural style. His collections were full of antique fragments and his home was piled high with unusual, and sometimes intriguing artefacts including Pharaoh Seti I's sarcophagus, marbles, friezes, casts, and wonderful classical statues of Apollo Belvedere and The Ephesian Diana.

Soane not only crammed these objects into every available space but also cleverly used mirrors and natural light to give rooms the illusion of being larger or brighter than they actually were. His eclectic style and love of paintings manifested itself in the Picture Room, with its moralistic series of paintings by Hogarth (*An Election* and *A Rake's Progress*) and stunning Venetian scenes by Canaletto. Here, to the delight of visitors, secretly hidden hinged-screen walls could open to reveal more paintings and architectural drawings as well as the Monk's Parlour below.

On his death Soane bequeathed his home and museum to the nation with the proviso that nothing would change. His instructions have been followed and the museum remains as quirky and flamboyant as when it was conceived. For more information refer to www.soane.org.

Above: The Model Room. (© Gareth Gardner)

Below: Sir John Soane's Museum frontage. (© Gareth Gardner)

10. Charles Dickens Museum, No. 48 Doughty Street

Run by the charitable trust, the Dickens Fellowship, the museum has practically become a site of pilgrimage for thousands of Charles Dickens (1812–70) fans, researchers and academics. Filled with more than 100,000 objects relating to the novelist, it is the most important Dickens collection throughout the world. Here you will find first editions, manuscripts, handwritten drafts from the novels he wrote, as well as personal items such as his beloved desk, cigar cutter, letters, snuffbox and quill pen. The museum also exhibits portraits of the author and his family, cartoons and illustrations from Dickens's novels.

No. 48 Doughty Street was leased by Dickens in 1837 when he was a little-known author, but by the time he moved from the house in late 1839, his reputation had grown significantly and he had become a household name. Three of his major works were written while he lived here: *The Pickwick Papers, Oliver Twist* and *Nicholas Nickleby,* and he had begun work on his final unfinished book, *The Mystery of Edwin Drood*.

The house, set in a private gated road with liveried porters, was certainly a move up the ladder for Dickens and his wife Catherine and it is the only one of his London homes that still remains. It is a typical terraced house of the period set over four floors with servant quarters and kitchens in the basement and a dining

Charles Dickens Museum.
(© Charles Dickens Museum)

Above: Charles Dickens's Study. (© Charles Dickens Museum)

Left: *Nicholas Nickleby* manuscript page. (© Charles Dickens Museum)

room on the ground floor, the site of Dickens many celebrated dinner parties. Upstairs, you find the drawing room where Dickens would occasionally read his latest works to the household, the family bedrooms, and Dickens's book-lined study where he wrote his novels and articles, often by candlelight.

While living in Doughty Street the family grew from one to three children. This, together with Dickens's increasing success and affluence, was the impetus to move again, this time to the much larger Devonshire House in Marylebone. Memorabilia from his later properties is displayed within the museum and there is also a delightful garden café and gift shop in the basement. For further information see www.dickensmuseum.com.

11. Eastman Dental Institute, Gray's Inn Road

This is another of Bloomsbury's buildings that owes its existence to a philanthropist; in this instance to George Eastman, an American entrepreneur whose fortune was made through his Eastman Kodak camera company. In the mid-1920s, along with two dignitaries of the Royal Free Hospital, he provided substantial funds to set up a dental and oral health clinic for central London's poor and disadvantaged children. The Eastman Dental Hospital opened on the Gray's Inn Road in 1931 and functioned as a department of the Royal Free Hospital providing routine treatment. Here, local children and adults were given free dental care and treatment for cleft lips and palate surgery. The clinic was built and operated on similar lines to the clinic that Eastman had set up in his home town, Rochester, USA, and played a very great role in the advancement of modern public dental healthcare in the UK.

With the founding of the National Health Service in 1948 the clinic became an independent dental hospital offering specialist rather than routine dental care.

Eastman Dental Institute.
(© A. McMurdo)

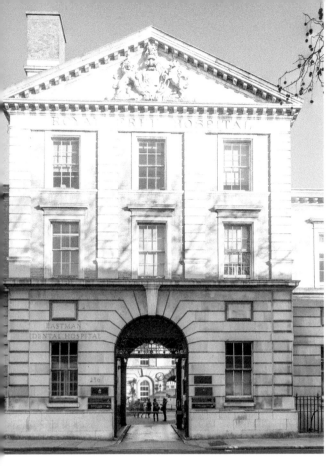

Eastman Dental Institute.
(© A. McMurdo)

Forty years later, after the Royal Free moved to new premises, the Eastman took over the entire hospital complex. Today, it is renowned as a specialist medical institution and a leading European centre of dental research. The hospital, now under the auspices of University College London, is an academic centre for postgraduate dentistry and renamed the Eastman Dental Institute. Its students study many courses ranging from diplomas to master's degrees and doctorates.

Interestingly, the site where the hospital is located was first built in 1812 as barracks for the Light Horse Volunteers. As such it was laid out as a quadrangle surrounded by four blocks and had a very grand entrance arch topped with a British lion. Despite alterations and additions to the buildings over the past 200 years the general layout remains almost unchanged. The Eastman's adjacent 1930s premises are built in the French-American Beaux Arts style and designed by Sir John Burnet and Thomas Tait.

12. Heal's, Tottenham Court Road

Undeniably one of London's most celebrated furniture stores, Heal's has been a major presence on Tottenham Court Road for over 200 years. John Harris Heal, a feather dresser by trade, first set up his business in 1810. After moving to his

Heal's.
(© A. McMurdo)

new premises here he turned his hand to furniture manufacture, and was soon selling bedding, lighting and furnishings as well. It was at Heal's that Londoners first discovered feather-filled mattresses, and they came flocking to buy these state-of-the-art beds. From the start, Heal's was at the forefront of its trade, selling quality merchandise of the most modern design. The store was also proactive in branding and marketing its products, seizing the opportunity to get its name more widely known by becoming one of the earliest retailers to place advertisements on book jackets at a time when paperbound books were flooding the market. Always keen to be an innovator, it supported and promoted contemporary British

Heal's. (© A. McMurdo)

furniture designs. In the early 1890s Ambrose Heal Jr, grandson of the founder, joined the company. He was a sound businessman and furniture designer and contributed greatly to the success of the store. In 1917 he opened the Mansard Gallery, Heal's own art gallery, where in 1919 Matisse, Picasso and Modigliani displayed their art for the first time in Britain.

During wartime (1939–45) Heal's workshop staff spent many hours sewing parachutes in support of the war effort. So expert did they become that the store subsequently introduced its own fabrics department once peace was declared. Although Heal's quality workmanship has much international acclaim, the store felt honoured to be commissioned by Buckingham Palace to restore its banqueting table in 1977.

Walk past Heal's today and glance up at its façade, which was designed by Ambrose's cousin, Cecil Brewer. A superb example of early twentieth-century shop architecture, it is especially noted for its frieze panels promoting the shop's wares ('The Sign of the Four Poster, Chairmakers, Upholstery'). Although no longer run as a family concern, the store continues to sell contemporary home furnishings of the very highest quality and design.

13. St Pancras Church, Euston Road

One of the first Greek Revival churches to be built in London, St Pancras is claimed to be the finest of its type. It is especially renowned for its splendid caryatids (draped female figures) facing out on to the busy Euston Road and its elegant octagonal tower crowning the portico of the building. At a time when Greece and its antiquities were becoming much better known, the church authorities selected designs presented in this fashionable style by father and son William and Henry Inwood. The latter, having recently visited the Temple of the Winds and the Erechtheum in Athens, took inspiration from these ancient monuments and included features from them to adorn and decorate the church exterior. Built in brick, Portland stone and terracotta, the church ultimately cost a staggering amount (nearly £77,000) and was the most expensive church building to be erected since the early 1700s.

Certainly (1822), when it was built the church would have been a most unusual sight with its terracotta caryatids guarding the crypt; it would have seemed foreign and marked the building out. Today, it is recognised by English Heritage for its outstanding architectural style (awarded Grade I listing), and over time has blended well into the urban landscape in which it sits. The interior of the church is striking too, not only for its magnitude but for its giant scagliola columns in the apse and the gallery supported by elegant lotus columns.

St Pancras possesses wonderful acoustics and regular lunchtime recitals take place here. The church hosts a music festival each year and events such as art exhibitions, filming and performances take place in the Crypt Gallery. Currently

Above: St Pancras
Church.
(© A. McMurdo)

Right: Caryatids,
St Pancras
Church.
(© A. McMurdo)

SAINT PANCRAS
PARISH CHURCH
Church of England
Anglican Communion

there is a magnificent garden installation by sculptor David Breuer-Weil. Made up of two gigantic bronze figures in humanoid shape the artist aims to demonstrate themes of belonging and isolation.

The present church has replaced the earlier Old St Pancras Church near to St Pancras station. Mary Woolstonecraft, author of *Frankenstein*, and the eminent architect Sir John Soane are both buried in the old churchyard.

14. Gordon Square, WC1

Gordon Square, forming one of a pair with Tavistock Square, is today largely occupied by the University of London. It was the last of seven squares to be built on the Duke of Bedford's estate in the early nineteenth century. The highly successful Thomas Cubitt (1788–1855), architect and man heralded for being the first to employ workers of all trades under his management, was commissioned by the estate to design the square. However, in the time it took to build, architectural styles moved on and Cubitt's original plans were altered affecting its overall uniformity. Nonetheless, the houses were similar in design and by repeating the formula of separate houses along the terraces his vision of harmony was upheld.

From the start an address in Gordon Square attracted the middle and upper middle classes, yet it was never able to compete with the more fashionable and centrally located Mayfair or Belgravia. In time, some of the residences gave way

Gordon Square. (© A. McMurdo)

Above: Bloomsbury Group
plaque, Gordon Square.
(© A. McMurdo)

Right: Town houses,
Gordon Square.
(© A. McMurdo)

to institutions and some were divided up, which changed the atmosphere of the square and encouraged new types of resident. The most famous perhaps of these were Vanessa (Bell), Virginia (Woolf) and Thoby and Adrian Stephen, who moved to No. 46 in 1904, from the more conventional Kensington, after the death of their father, Sir Leslie Stephen. Perhaps rebelling against the norms of their parents' generation, the siblings chose to lead unconventional lives. They were politically liberal, free-thinking, artistic and intellectual and held meetings at their home for friends and like-minded individuals. Artists, painters, philosophers, economists and writers such as Roger Fry, Duncan Grant, Clive Bell, Leonard Woolf, Lytton Strachey, John Maynard Keynes and E. M. Forster attended the Thursday and Friday sessions regularly and became known as the Bloomsbury Group. Notorious for flaunting all conventions, for their sexuality and relationships, they were cleverly described as 'couples living in squares but loving in triangles'. Interestingly, a century on, they remain an intrinsic part of Bloomsbury's appeal and its association with literature and art. Much has been written about them and their influence on the area.

15. Woburn Walk, WC1

This picture card thoroughfare is a real world away from the streets that surround it. Nestled between hotels on Upper Woburn Place, it is all too easy to pass by. Today, Woburn Walk is pedestrianised and contains a range of upmarket shops ranging from wedding dress salons to newsagents and cafés. It consists of two low terraces of shops with wooden curved bay-fronted windows, and has a row of old-fashioned lamp posts and trees running through the middle of the tiny street. It is an especially pretty enclave in spring when the trees are in blossom.

Above and below: Woburn Walk. (© A. McMurdo)

Built in 1822 as a shopping street, it was purposely placed near the boundary of the Bedford Estate so as not to disturb the well-to-do residents! The terraces, designed by the architect Thomas Cubitt (1788–1855), were built to accommodate, then as now, shops and housing. Towards the end of the nineteenth century the hugely successful Irish poet and Nobel Prize winner William Butler Yeats (1865–1939) lived at No. 5, holding regular weekly meetings in his home with the popular poets T. S. Eliot and John Masefield.

Naturally, Woburn Walk is a popular film location, most recently seen in the TV series *Unforgotten*.

16. British Museum, Great Russell Street

To visit the British Museum is to experience life in every continent of the globe. This truly international museum is full of wonderful displays ranging from coins and clocks to ceramics, antiquities, artworks, sculpture, jewellery, carvings, mosaics and centuries-old silver hoards. Based in the very heart of Bloomsbury, it is close to both London's West End and the campus area of the University of London. The museum is rightfully hailed as one of the capital's top attractions and is especially renowned for its breathtaking Egyptian, Greek and Roman galleries. Here you will see hieroglyphics and painted sarcophagi, marble wall carvings, statuary, mosaics and even the mummified body of a man thought to have died in the desert around 3,500 BC. A particular prize of the museum is the Rosetta Stone,

Main entrance of the British Museum. (© A. McMurdo)

Above: Entrance to King Edward VII Galleries, the British Museum. (© A. McMurdo)

Below: The British Museum, Great Russell Street. (© A. McMurdo)

with its text written in three scripts: hieroglyphics, Egyptian demotic and Ancient Greek. Only when scholars realised that the text of each language was the same that scholars were able to decipher the hieroglyphics – a language that had been lost for around 1,400 years.

The British Museum was established in the mid-eighteenth century at a time of world discovery when intrepid travellers returned home with every type of treasure and previously unknown animals and flora. It owes its existence to Hans Sloane (1666–1753), a physician and naturalist who had amassed an enormous collection of objects during his travels in the Caribbean. He bequeathed this to the nation on his death (securing a payment of £20,000 for his heirs), and the museum opened in 1759. As the collections grew the museum increased in size. Now there are areas devoted to the Islamic World, the Orient, Africa, Asia, the Americas, Saxons and Vikings and so much more! With the opening of the Great Court in 2000 the museum is much lighter and more spacious, and large temporary exhibitions are now displayed in the new World Conservation and Exhibitions Centre. One visit is really never enough and you are sure to leave wanting to return. Refer to www.britishmuseum.org for details of opening hours and current exhibitions.

17. Wilkins Building, University College London (UCL), Gower Street

Set behind a narrow gateway on Gower Street the neoclassical Wilkins Building, with its imposing Corinthian column portico and green dome, rises above a flight of stone stairs at the rear of the courtyard. Its style may seem familiar as its designer, William Wilkins (1778–1839), was also the architect of the National Gallery in Trafalgar Square. Initially the college was known as the University of London, but changed its name to UCL on the award of its charter in 1836. Although the main central range of Wilkins' architectural plan was built in 1827, it was not until 1985 that the building was fully completed and then not to Wilkins' original designs.

The founders of the university were mainly a group of freethinkers who believed in education for all regardless of one's faith, race or creed, and were greatly inspired by the philosopher Jeremy Bentham. Their institution, unlike the universities of Oxford and Cambridge, would admit men and women equally and offer new courses to students in subjects such as science and modern languages, as well as the traditional curriculum of mathematics and the classics. This new secular approach to education gave rise to the institution being dubbed 'the Godless College on Gower Street'.

Nonetheless, the college thrived and its student body grew. By the mid-1830s, it joined with its Anglican rival, King's College, to become constituent colleges of the University of London, a degree-awarding body and responsible for student examinations. Today UCL has more than 38,000 students and employs in excess

Above and left: The Wilkins Building, UCL. (© A. McMurdo)

of 13,000 staff. It has many celebrated former alumni as well as twenty-nine Nobel Prize laureates among its numbers.

An unusual relic to be found within the building is Jeremy Bentham's Auto-Icon ('man in his own image'). Set in a wooden cabinet, it is Bentham's preserved skeleton, dressed in his own clothes and seated in a pensive stance. The body is padded out with straw, and the head made of wax. Certainly worth a view if you are passing by www.ucl.ac.uk.

18. Great Ormond Street Hospital for Children (GOSH), Great Ormond Street and Guilford Street

This internationally renowned hospital began life in 1852 as a place for children to access dedicated inpatient care and medical attention. With no similar institution in the UK at the time its establishment was a massive step forward. In the 160 or so years since it opened GOSH has gone from strength to strength, and has been involved in major medical and surgical breakthroughs and much

Great Ormond Street Hospital.
(© A. McMurdo)

Above: Great Ormond Street Hospital.
(© A. McMurdo)

Left: Mittal Children's Medical
Centre, Great Ormond Street Hospital.
(© A. McMurdo)

pioneering treatment. Not only has it spearheaded research into paediatric medicine but has also been greatly involved in the field of paediatric child psychiatry, and the treatment of child leukaemia and cancer. Transplants of the heart, the lungs and bone marrow were pioneered here in the 1960s and 1970s and since 2001 GOSH has been the only centre worldwide to offer heart valve replacements without the need for open surgery.

In order to continue with its ground-breaking research, acquire new and often expensive machinery and to provide the most modern operating theatres, intensive care beds and wards, GOSH relies upon donations. It receives one-off, regular and corporate gift payments and is heavily involved in fundraising activity. Its charity website www.gosh.org identifies ways of helping the hospital and runs a programme of events to raise money such as half-marathons, charity skydives and even an office tower climb.

Since 1929 when J. M. Barrie gifted the copyright of *Peter Pan* to the hospital GOSH has enjoyed a regular income but when the original copyright expired in 1987 there was great concern about the hospital's future. Thankfully, Parliament passed a unique amendment to the Copyright Act that enabled it to continue to receive royalties in perpetuity in the UK from Barrie's book and play.

GOSH today sprawls over a vast site with a wide range of architectural styles. Fortunately, generous donations are received and funds raised for new buildings and vital facilities; the Mittal Children's Centre is the most recent to open in 2018 and is shortly to be followed by the Zayed Centre for Research into Rare Disease in Children.

19. Church of Christ the King, Gordon Square

Situated beside Torrington Square, Bloomsbury's pedestrianised campus of the University of London, you cannot fail to notice this splendid building. The Church of Christ the King stands out not simply for its size and scale but also for its beautiful Bath stone and neo-Gothic appearance. Understandably nicknamed 'the cathedral of Bloomsbury', it is renowned for its Early English Gothic exterior and Decorated interior as well as the highly carved English Chapel at the east end of the church. When it was opened in 1853 it was considered to be one of England's most magnificent churches of the period.

It was designed by Raphael Brandon specifically for the Catholic Apostolic Church, a sect that believed in the Second Coming of Christ. They were often referred to as the 'Irvingites', named after their charismatic leader, Edward Irving, a Scottish clergyman. By the dawn of the twentieth century the church had lost much of its original appeal when its prophecies failed to materialise. Subsequently, its membership fell and today the order has practically died out.

From 1963 to 1994 the building became the 'University Church of Christ the King' serving the University of London's Anglican chaplaincy. Many of London's

Above: Church of Christ the King. (© A. McMurdo)

Below: The English Chapel, Church of Christ the King. (© A. McMurdo)

students worshipped here. In 1983 a memorial service was held in the church for the celebrated architectural historian Nikolaus Pevsner. Nowadays an Anglican group, Forward in Faith, holds services in the English Chapel, and opens the chapel for private prayer on weekdays.

Adjacent to the church is Dr Williams's Library, an impressive mock-Tudor building. The doctor, a respected minister in Ireland, left his collection (more than 7,500 books) as a library for theological students on his death in 1716. Over the years the library moved a number of times before settling into its present premises, a former student hall of residence, in 1890.

In 2006, the library made world headlines for selling its prize possession, an almost perfect copy of Shakespeare's *First Folio* containing all thirty-six of Shakespeare's plays. Selling for £2.8 million at Sotheby's, it was the most valuable printed book ever sold at their London auction house.

20. James Smith & Sons, New Oxford Street

James Smith & Sons is undoubtedly one of Bloomsbury's great gems and a superb example of what an upmarket shop would have looked like in the Victorian age. It was and is still a shop entirely filled with the most British of products, the indispensable umbrella. The shop is said to be the oldest of its kind in Europe and has been supplying customers with its vast, interesting range of umbrellas and accessories for almost 200 years. Based in its New Oxford Street home since 1857, the interior is scarcely unchanged. Then, as now, craftsmen produce new designs and repair broken umbrellas in the on-site cellar workshop.

James
Smith & Sons.
(© A. McMurdo)

It is certainly difficult to pass the shop without being tempted by its stunning window displays of umbrellas for every occasion. They are an exciting kaleidoscope of intense colours and patterns, with every conceivable type of umbrella on show. Above the windows wonderful nineteenth-century signs advertise umbrellas for men, for women, for golf, for the garden as well as tropical sunshades. Still on offer today you also find a large assortment of walking and seat sticks for sale within the shop.

Right from the start James Smith & Sons was a great success. It became even more so once the lightweight steel frame was invented in 1851. This increased the popularity of the umbrella greatly as earlier styles had been made of wood and as such were heavy and difficult to close when damp. Umbrellas then became sought-after products. With such a buoyant market James Smith opened several new shops in London supplying many dignitaries including Prime Minister Gladstone.

Nowadays, this is the only one of its nineteenth-century shops to remain. Its survival in the modern age is quite extraordinary especially when an umbrella can cost anything up to £1,750! But for those who want the crème de la crème, umbrellas fashioned from the very best of woods, and manufactured to suit their height, this will always be the place to come.

James Smith & Sons.
(© A. McMurdo)

James Smith & Sons. (© A. McMurdo)

21. The Princess Louise, High Holborn

The Princess Louise is quintessentially an English High Victorian public house, first built in 1872 and remodelled in 1891. It underwent a thorough refurbishment in 2007 when it was returned to its former glory. The pub takes its name from Queen Victoria's fourth daughter, Louise, Duchess of Argyll, who was considered a beauty. Also a celebrated artist and sculptor, it was she who designed the imposing statue of her mother outside Kensington Palace.

The pub has the most striking interior and is a wonderful example of true Victorian craftsmanship. With mosaic floors, stuccoed ceiling, ornate mirrors, magnificent wood panelling and embossed and engraved glasswork, it reflects the greatness, grandeur and importance of the British Empire in the late nineteenth century. The artisans who produced the furniture and decorations were of the highest calibre with hand-painted tiles being supplied by W. B. Simpson & Sons, and French embossed glass by R. Morris & Son. The remarkably grand central

Above and below: Princess Louise. (© A. McMurdo)

Princess Louise. (© A. McMurdo)

island bar has columns topped with Corinthian capitals, and an exquisite wooden arch, displaying a clock and finials above. Several private booths surround the bar and each is characterised by dark wood and etched glass partitions. Customers exit these through an elaborately carved screen into a narrow corridor that is awash with embellished mirrors, a frieze and wonderful Victorian wall tiling. The gentlemen's toilets, with marble urinals, are equally as opulent. These are now listed, which prevents them from being destroyed or modified.

In many respects, the pub interior is reminiscent of a former 'gin palace' so common at the height of the British Empire, but this was a pub that always sold ale. The tradition continues and today the Princess Louise is tied to the Samuel Smith Brewery so only sells the brewery's products. The pub is certainly one of the most attractive in the area and is popular with local office workers and tourists. To see it at its best make sure you visit at off-peak times when you will get a seat and be able to appreciate its wonderful delights.

22. Cabmen's Shelter, Russell Square

A much-loved part of transport heritage, the green cabmen's shelter is one of only thirteen such huts left on London's streets today and remains very dear to cab drivers and locals alike.

The introduction of the brightly painted hut to the street scene goes back to the 1870s when horse-drawn hansom cabs were the main form of transport on

Cabmen's Shelter. (© A. McMurdo)

the streets. The cabman's lot was hard; he worked in all weathers yet could not legally leave his vehicle unattended. If he needed to leave his cab to find a bite to eat he would have to pay someone to guard the cab. Many cabbies would visit the nearest public house and then be tempted to have an alcoholic drink or two while there, rendering them unfit to drive and frustrated customers would be unable to find a sober driver.

This state of affairs led to the establishment of the Cabmen's Shelter Fund by a group of aristocrats led by the philanthropic 7th Earl of Shaftesbury. Within no time a number of timber-framed huts appeared around the city, designated as cabbie shelters, a place for the drivers to find warmth and refreshment. The huts, following Metropolitan Police guidelines, were a standard size, no larger than a horse and cart, as they were situated on the public highways. Strict rules applied within them that banned the practice of gambling, the drinking of alcohol and swearing, and only qualified cabbies were allowed inside (a rule that still applies today).

In recent times the owners, the Worshipful Company of Hackney Carriage Drivers, have struck a deal with Universal Studios allowing them to use the Cabmen Shelter design at Universal's Harry Potter Attraction. This has provided much-needed funds to put towards the maintenance of these characterful Grade II listed huts.

Cabmen's Shelter. (© A. McMurdo)

Although only placed in Russell Square in 1987, this cabmen's shelter is already one of Bloomsbury's most welcoming and loved landmarks. Every day people buy snacks at the shelter's window hatch and many stop to take photos of this quirky reminder of times gone by.

23. National Hospital for Neurology and Neurosurgery, Queen Square

The founding in 1859 of the National Hospital for the Paralysed and Epileptic was an enormous, innovative step forward in the treatment of disorders of the nervous system. It was the very first hospital in the country to address these conditions and due to its private funding, was able to offer free treatment and charge only those people wealthy enough to pay. Up until this time many who suffered from neurological disorders would find themselves confined to the workhouse, hidden away from the normal world, subjected to extremely harsh living conditions and with no real access to treatment.

The National Hospital for Neurology, as the hospital subsequently became known, was the first of many to appear in Queen Square and from the start was referred to as the National. It attracted the most eminent physicians of the day and it was their many written neurological contributions and pioneering techniques in neurological and neurosurgical therapy that established the hospital's reputation.

Above: National Hospital for Neurology and Neurosurgery. (© A. McMurdo)

Below: Eentrance plaque, National Hospital for Neurology and Neurosurgery. (© A. McMurdo)

As the National's standing grew so did its site. During the early 1880s a new wing, designed by the architects M. P. Manning and J. Simpson, was constructed. This remains the main hospital building, easily identified by its warm red-brick façade and built in the distinctive French Renaissance style. Its symmetry and

Gable end, National
Hospital for Neurology
and Neurosurgery.
(© A. McMurdo)

features are extremely attractive with much terracotta decoration. The main
entrance porch, recessed verandas, pediments and windows all demonstrate
wonderful craftsmanship. Interestingly, John Simpson, one of its architects, was
later responsible for the design of the original 1923 Wembley Stadium.

The hospital remained independent until 1948 when the National Health
Service was formed. Today, it is part of the University College London Hospital
NHS Foundation Trust and is known as the National Hospital for Neurology
and Neurosurgery. As the largest institution of its kind in the UK it has a range
of specialised units that deal with conditions affecting the spinal cord, the brain
and the general nervous system. It is highly regarded worldwide as a centre of
excellence specialising in clinical care, research and training.

24. Peabody Buildings, Herbrand Street

The Society for Improving the Conditions of the Labouring Classes established its
'Model Houses for Families' in Streatham Street beside the British Museum thirty-
five years before the Herbrand Street flats were built. The society's five-storey
blocks were built in yellow stock brick and appeared quite forbidding, but the flats
themselves were spacious with two bedrooms, a scullery, toilet and living room.
Undoubtedly, they were a great improvement on the tenants' previous homes.
Lord Ashley (later to become the Earl of Shaftesbury) lead the society and was
one of a group of nineteenth-century reformers including Angela Burdett-Coutts,

Above and left:
Peabody Buildings,
Herbrand Street.
(© A. McMurdo)

Charles Dickens and George Peabody who worked tirelessly in Victorian times to improve the conditions of poor and decent working people.

George Peabody (1795–1869) was a wealthy American merchant banker who had settled in London in 1837. Walking around the city's street he was greatly moved by the extreme poverty he observed and this led him to donate £500,000 of his money to create dwellings for respectable, yet poor, working-class people. Prospective Peabody tenants were strictly vetted and only those in steady jobs were offered accommodation. The flats were not only solidly built, but well ventilated and offered shared sanitary facilities, laundries, bathhouses, coal stores as well as safe children's play areas. The Herbrand Street Estate opened in 1885 and was originally built as eight blocks surrounding a central courtyard with 450 rooms in 205 dwellings. Strict rules governed tenancies: each resident had to be vaccinated against smallpox and take turns in cleaning the communal passages and lavatories. Generally, residents worked within walking distance of the estate and would probably have been employed as labourers, printers, tailors, shop assistants, coachmen and printers.

On Peabody's death in 1869 he was given a state funeral in Westminster Abbey and his body was interred there. Yet, once the terms of his will were revealed his body was exhumed and, in accordance with his wishes, returned to Danvers, his home town, which subsequently renamed itself Peabody. His legacy continues and today more than 70,000 Londoners reside in Peabody accommodation.

25. Dairy Supply Company Ltd, No. 30 Coptic Street and No. 35 Little Russell Street

At the junction of Coptic Street and Little Russell Street one is unexpectedly faced with the most wonderful example of late Victorian architecture. The two adjoining buildings were constructed in 1888 for the Dairy Supply Company Ltd, and designed by the architect R. P. Whellock. He not only created the fine-looking buildings but embellished the façades with historic inscription, thus advertising the dairy's premises making it clear for all to see. Built in yellow stock brick, common in London at the time, the buildings are made more attractive by the use of banded red-brick and stone dressings, delightful round-arched windows and much ornamentation in the form of shells, a milk churn and even a sunflower motif.

George Barham (1836–1913), the founder of the company, was a most enterprising businessman; in the 1860s when wholesale milk production was suffering badly due to the outbreak of cattle plague, he set up a highly successful supply system. Importing milk from Derbyshire farms, he was soon able to provide milk to 50 per cent of London's market. To insure the company against market competition he branched out into the manufacture of dairy utensils and

Above: Dairy Supply Company. (© A. McMurdo)

Below left: Dairy Supply Company. (© A. McMurdo)

Below right: Milk churn relief, Dairy Supply Company. (© A. McMurdo)

the Bloomsbury dairy subsequently became the first major producer of dairy equipment. One of the company's key items invented by Barham himself was the galvanised iron milk churn, specifically designed for rail transportation.

The dairy finally moved out of the premises following the Second World War, when Little Russell Street's warehouse and laboratory were converted into office space and No. 30 Coptic Street was snapped up in 1967 by the up-and-coming restaurant business Pizza Express. This was the company's second restaurant and like the first in Soho was marked by its open kitchen and casual dining. Great care in the redesign of the building from dairy to restaurant was taken by Enzo Apicella, allowing for much of its early character to be retained and visitors can still see the original wall tiling, black and white marble floor and art nouveau details.

26. Former Russell Hotel, Russell Square

This stunning eight-storey building, dominating Russell Square, was built as the Russell Hotel in the late nineteenth century. Designed by Charles Fitzroy Doll (1850–1929), surveyor to the Bedford Estate, it is a marvellous example of French Renaissance architecture and true to Doll's reputation, it is particularly ornate with an array of statuary, garlands and friezes. Its exterior is red brick, clad with terracotta in the thé-au-lait (tea with milk) style of the period with gables above

Entrance hall of Kimpton Fitzroy Hotel, formerly the Russell Hotel. (© Tom Mannion)

Above and left: Kimpton Fitzroy Hotel, formerly the Russell Hotel. (© A. McMurdo)

and grand turrets at either corner. High above its main entrance are two distinctive conical roofs covered in green fish scale tiles while on the first floor, four life-size statues of the English queens, Elizabeth I, Mary, Anne and Victoria, appear in niches, the work of sculptor Henry Charles Fehr (1867–1940), known for his sculptures on the Supreme Court in Parliament Square. The elaborate decoration includes coats of arms of countries around the globe and cute cherubs can be seen on the façade as well as on the lamp posts outside the building.

Inside, the hotel has always been known for its opulence, especially the lobby and staircase areas, magnificently adorned in French and Italian marble. When first built, the bedrooms with en-suite facilities were considered avant-garde and the dining areas and lounges all exuded a great feeling of luxury, rather like the grand ocean liners of the day. Doll not only designed the original sumptuous hotel restaurant, but also, a decade or so later, one for the ill-fated liner RMS *Titanic*, supposed to be a replica of it. In fact, the saying 'to be dolled up' is said to have its origin in Doll and his use of lavish decoration.

Most recently, following a change of ownership the hotel underwent a major refurbishment by design architects Tara Bernerd & Partners. Once again returned to its former magnificence, it was subsequently rebranded as the Kimpton Fitzroy London Hotel. Despite its name change for many it remains a great Bloomsbury landmark and no doubt will continue to be referred to as the Russell Hotel.

27. University College London Hospital (UCLH), Gower Street and Euston Road

Since 2005 UCLH has been based in a purpose-built twenty-first-century hospital on the Euston Road, just a stone's throw away from its previous home in Gower Street. It is part of the UCL Hospitals NHS Foundation Trust and is spread over five hospitals in Central London yet still very closely linked to UCL. The present building, designed by Llewelyn Davies Yeang (2005) to be a state-of-the-art teaching hospital as well as a major centre for medical research, is easily recognised by its green and white panel exterior and imposing seventeen-storey tower.

UCLH, as one of London's main hospitals, not only has an extremely busy Accident and Emergency department, but is also highly involved in the care of cancer and stroke patients, general surgery, and possesses the largest critical care unit in the NHS. It has recently been selected as one of two hospital sites in the UK to provide the innovative proton beam therapy and a new building dedicated to the treatment is due to open in 2020.

For most of the twentieth century, the hospital occupied the Cruciform Building in Gower Street, designed by the Victorian architect Alfred Waterhouse (1830–1905). It is a magnificent building in the shape of St Andrew's cross, and is conspicuous for its red-brick and terracotta façade, soaring turrets and towers. An excellent example of Gothic Revival architecture, the building is full of intricate

Left: New building
of University College
London Hospital.
(© A. McMurdo)

Below: Cruciform
and new buildings,
University College
London Hospital.
(© A. McMurdo)

Cruciform building, University
College London Hospital.
(© A. McMurdo)

decoration and bears similarities to Waterhouse's other works at the Natural
History Museum and Holborn Bars. It is now home to the Wolfson Institute for
Biomedical Research and UCL's Medical School's pre-clinical training facility.

An earlier university hospital occupied the site from 1834 until the development
of the Cruciform Building in the early 1900s. It was the very first university
hospital in London and interestingly founded because the university needed
to provide its medical students with clinical practice, denied to them by other
medical institutions on account of the university's 'godless' status (q.v. Wilkins
Building, University College London).

28. Mary Ward House, Tavistock Place

Mary Ward (1851–1920) was a member of the celebrated Arnold family, whose
grandfather had been the headmaster of Rugby School and her uncle, the poet
Matthew Arnold. A bestselling novelist in her own right she wrote under the name
Mrs Humphrey Ward and was a great believer in the education of women and in
social justice and equality.

The Mary Ward House. (© A. McMurdo)

Mary Ward was conscious of the social problems, urban poverty and lack of opportunities for many in the Bloomsbury district so in the 1890s planned to build her own 'Settlement' to provide cultural and educational opportunities for ordinary people. She began fundraising and gained financial support towards the building from the radical philanthropist John Passmore Edwards, while the landowner, the Duke of Bedford, donated the land. The institution, when it began in 1897, was named Passmore Edwards Settlement after its main benefactor, only changing title to Mary Ward Settlement following Mary's death.

From the day it opened the building was considered to be one of the most attractive examples of Arts and Craft architecture in London. Designed by two young architects, Smith and Brewer, its warm red-brick façade, interesting arches, curved windows, stone entrances and canopies work together to make the building a visual treat. It is no wonder that it has been awarded Grade I listing on English Heritage's register of listed buildings.

The Mary Ward House. (© A. McMurdo)

Once the Settlement was up and running, Mary turned her hand to other projects; she set up the very first play centre for children and went on to establish after-school and school holiday activities for them. She also opened the very first school for disabled children in the Settlement in 1899.

The premises remained occupied by the Mary Ward Settlement until the early 1980s when the organisation moved and the building was relaunched as a conference and exhibition centre. Now its original basement gymnasium has become an airy flexible space and is used for conferences, art exhibitions, training workshops and for filming and product launches.

29. The Lady Ottoline, Northington Street

This fine building is most aptly named after one of Bloomsbury's most celebrated society hostesses and patrons, Lady Ottoline Violet Anne Cavendish-Bentinck. An aristocrat by birth, first cousin to Elizabeth Bowes Lyon (later to become the Queen Mother), and the great-great-niece of the Duke of Wellington, she was

The Lady Ottoline. (© A. McMurdo)

certainly very well connected in British society. The most striking of figures, unusually tall with a head of flaming copper hair, and outlandishly dressed in bright clothing, Lady Ottoline was hard to miss.

Both she and her MP husband were Liberals and had a string of extramarital affairs. She was passionate about the arts and became patron to many intellectuals, artists, poets, sculptors and authors, giving them much needed support and helping them to establish their careers. Lady Ottoline kept an open house in her Bedford Square town house, surrounding herself with clever men and women whose greatest passion was talk. Many of them, like their host, were pacifists, non-religious and with left-wing tendencies but they were all definite individuals, and not a closely-knit group. So, it would have been natural to come across T. S. Eliot, Augustus John, Henry James, Bertrand Russell, Virginia Woolf or any of the so-called Bloomsbury Group in her home; many of her circle used it as a club. Even when she moved into a more modest house in Gower Street after the war, she continued to open her doors, providing hospitality and friendship to all.

Today, The Lady Ottoline gastropub occupies a similar though considerably smaller town house than Lady Ottoline's Bedford Square residence, and in the manner of its namesake, extends a very warm welcome to customers with fine dining in elegant surroundings. The pub prides itself on its seasonal menu using fresh locally produced British food and is open every day offering special lunch time and Sunday menus. The downstairs bar serves an interesting range of cocktails as well as more than forty gins, a wide range of craft beers and real ales. Upstairs meals are served in the most genteel of settings.

30. The Italian Hospital, Queen Square

During the nineteenth century the area to the east of Queen Square was home to many Italians. The first wave of immigrants arrived following the Napoleonic Wars, and were craftsmen such as mosaicists, clock and watchmakers and picture framers. Their numbers swelled from 5,000 to 10,000 between 1851 and 1901 when they were joined by many less skilled workers, men who sold ice cream, played the accordion or were organ grinders and who were mainly very poor. It became evident that there was a need for an Italian hospital where the community could be treated and cared for by native Italian speakers.

Their plight was recognised by fellow countryman Commendatore Giovanni Ortelli, who was a successful businessman residing in Queen Square. He founded the Italian Hospital, which moved into its own premises in 1898. The hospital was funded by subscription in both Italy and Britain and open to all nationalities. It remained as an independent hospital until 1990 when it finally closed due to financial difficulties. Nowadays, it forms part of the nearby Great Ormond Street Hospital for Sick Children.

The Italian Hospital.
(© A. McMurdo)

31. Imagination, Store Street, South Crescent

This amazing signature building for the internationally renowned creative giants Imagination was designed by Archigram architect Ron Herron in the late 1980s. Herron was commissioned by the agency to develop a scheme for its head office building that was not only striking but would reflect the style and innovation of the company and provide a real wow factor. The site he had to transform consisted of a number of buildings: a six-storey Edwardian red-brick building, on South Crescent, along with several buildings behind it. Due to the nature of the company he needed to ensure that there was sufficient and appropriate space for media studios, events such as fashion shows, and for the many designers, photographers and consultants.

Herron's clever design retained the façade on South Crescent but gutted the interior of the old building. He then used a fabric tensile roof to connect the buildings at the front and back, resulting in the creation of one structure. In between them he developed a large, spacious atrium with lightweight walkways. The result was stunning, winning the UK's Building of the Year Award in 1991, and Imagination's tented roof remains a landmark of the area.

Imagination, South Crescent. (© Imagination)

Imagination rooftop with Senate House in background. (© Imagination)

32. Euston Fire Station, No. 172 Euston Road

This handsome building was designed in the fashionable Arts and Crafts style by London County Council's (LCC) architects and remains a wonderful testament to early twentieth-century civic architecture. The Arts and Crafts movement, greatly influenced by the designer William Morris (1834–96), sought the return to more traditional methods of construction and design and higher standards of craftsmanship. One glance at Euston fire station with its use of quality materials and decoration explains why it is considered to be of great architectural merit. Slightly set back from the main Euston Road, it is immediately recognisable due to the inscription above the appliance bays: 'LCC Fire Brigade Station Euston 1902'. The station was built as headquarters for the North Division of the London Fire Brigade, occupying just the ground level, and the station commander lived above in private quarters on the fourth floor.

Interestingly, a statutory London fire service did not exist until 1866. Prior to this outbreaks of fire were dealt with by individual fire insurance companies. Fire marks were placed on the company's buildings and firefighters only extinguished fires if they could identify the company's fire mark, frequently leaving uninsured properties to burn!

Euston fire station. (© A. McMurdo)

33. Royal Academy of Dramatic Art (RADA), Gower Street and Malet Street

You know you have reached RADA in Gower Street by its decorative main entrance. Here, two carved stone figures by the sculptor Alan Durst stand on either side of the doorway bearing masks representing Comedy and Tragedy.

RADA came to this building in 1905 shortly after its foundation by actor manager Sir Herbert Beerbohm Tree. It is one of the country's oldest drama schools and is a world leader in acting and theatre production. Its courses not only prepare students for careers on the stage, films, TV and radio but also in the art of stage management and technical craft specialisms. The academy has always been privately funded but a bequest from the playwright George Bernard Shaw has allowed RADA to remain on its original site and provide funds for the training of some of the profession's most talented writers and actors. Names like Kenneth Branagh, Richard Attenborough, Gemma Arterton, Alan Rickman, Tom Hiddleston, Lolita Chakrabarti, Clive Owen, Allison Janney, Ben Whishaw and Alex Kingston are but a few of an enormous list of great actors who have passed through RADA's doors.

Throughout its lifetime the building has been subject to reconstruction, most recently in 2000 when Avery Associates transformed what had been a cramped labyrinthine interior into a much lighter area enhancing the feeling of space.

Above: Gower Street entrance, Royal Accadamy of Dramatic Arts. (© A. McMurdo)

Right: Malet Street entrance, Royal Accadamy of Dramatic Arts. (© A. McMurdo)

Now occupying ten floors, the building is full of rehearsal, sound, dance and light studios as well as classrooms, acting studios, a scenic art workshop, costume workrooms and offices. Rehearsals and performances take place in RADA's three on-site theatres accessed from Malet Street: the Jerwood Vanbrugh Theatre with a 200-seat capacity, and the smaller George Bernard Shaw and John Gielgud studios. Other performances are held in the RADA Studios, Studio Theatre and Club Theatre, based in the former Drill Hall in nearby Chenies Street.

RADA today offers a number of higher education courses that are validated by King's College London. It is also an affiliate school of the Conservatoire for Dance and Drama.

34. Russell Square Underground Station, Bernard Street

Located right in the very heart of Bloomsbury, thousands of people pass through and by Russell Square Station every day. The station, with its wide frontage, Romanesque arches and semicircular windows is undoubtedly a wonderful example of Edwardian baroque architecture. Not surprising then

Above and below: Russell Square Underground Station. (© A. McMurdo)

that it is one of a handful of London Underground stations recognised by English Heritage for its architectural design and features and awarded Grade II listed status. The station was one of over forty designed by a young architect, Leslie Green (1875–1908), in the early 1900s, working under great pressure.

Green's employer, the Underground Electric Railways Ltd (UERL), was keen for him to create a distinctive corporate style on a fairly limited budget. His response was to construct the stations using strong steel frames and to clad the exterior with attractive eye-catching ox-blood faience tiles. Through his use of standardised signage and typeface as well as decoration in the popular Arts and Crafts and art nouveau styles he formed a real brand for the UERL that is still instantly recognisable today, and can be seen both at Russell Square station and other tube stations around the city.

35. Sicilian Avenue, WC1

What an unexpected delight to discover this charming Edwardian passageway running between Bloomsbury Square and Southampton Row. Not only a useful cut-through, the avenue also provides a flavour of Italy and the classical world amid the bustling urban street scene. Lined with chic, sophisticated shops, the

Below left and right: Sicilian Avenue. (© A. McMurdo)

pedestrianised street has an air of outdoor living and is the ideal place to come to people watch, especially in summertime.

The entrances at either end are grand; open screens made up of Ionic columns and the name 'Sicilian Avenue' emblazoned in gold-leaf above the gateways. Designed by R. J. Worley, architect to the Bedford Estate, the avenue is highly decorative with ornate pillars and projecting bay windows. Today offices are accommodated above the shops but these beautifully adorned buildings were once residential apartments. Look up to see the rich red-brick and white terracotta ornamentation as well as the fabulous upper-storey curved turrets. Why 'Sicilian' Avenue? There is no definitive answer, but possibly a trip to Sicily in the early 1900s by the landowner, the 11th Duke of Bedford, was the inspiration for its name.

36. Grant Museum of Zoology, Rockefeller Building, University Street

The splendid and most impressive Rockefeller Building with its grand Ionic columns, pavilions and warm red brick stands only metres away from UCH's Crucible Building, yet both were surprisingly designed by the same architectural practice. Completed within a year of each other, the Crucible Building owes its design to Alfred Waterhouse (1830–1905), while the Rockefeller Building to his son, Paul (1861–1924), proving perhaps how different generations are always keen to develop their own, and new, architectural styles.

The part of the building that now houses the Grant Museum of Zoology was the original UCH Medical School library and has been home to the museum's collections since 2011. When the library first closed, the space was used in a variety of ways and even featured in the 2005 movie *Batman Begins*, serving as a courtroom in Gotham City.

In certain respects, on entering the museum you might think you are walking into a film set as there is a definite feeling of a bygone era. The interior, on two floors, is full of wood and glass cabinets, stuffed to the brim with all manner of specimens. There are skeletons, skulls, bones, glass and wax models, mammoth tusks, mounted animals and even a Galapagos tortoise shell. In total there are 68,000 objects in today's collection. They relate to the entire animal kingdom and have arrived at the museum from many sources, although the original collection belonged to Robert Grant (1793–1874), UCL's first professor of Zoology and Comparative Anatomy, after whom the museum is named.

Many of the display specimens are in glass jars and often preserved in fluid. Two extremely rare specimens are the skeleton of the extinct quagga, a zebra from South Africa, and the massive antlers and skull of the giant deer, extinct for more than 7,000 years. The vast collection including dodo bones, the skeleton of one of the world's longest snakes and even a 508-million-year-old fossil worm is fascinating and a visit to the museum a great experience. For opening times see www.ucl.ac.uk.

Above: Grant Museum of Zoology, Gower Street. (© A. McMurdo)

Below: Gallery in the Grant Museum of Zoology. (© A. McMurdo)

Quagga skeleton, Grant Museum of Zoology. (© A. McMurdo)

37. Waterstones, Torrington Place and Gower Street

Charles Fitzroy Doll (1850–1929) designed this wonderfully ornate and flamboyant building constructed in 1907–08. At the time it was developed as a terrace of shops and apartments and was a joint venture between the landowners, the University of London, and private developers. Nowadays it accommodates just one shop, the booksellers Waterstones, and offices have replaced residential accommodation.

Doll trained under the distinguished Victorian architect Sir Matthew Digby Wyatt, and worked alongside him during the 1860s on the design of the India Office in Whitehall. Twenty years later he was appointed surveyor to the Bedford Estate and became renowned for his work on hotels (q.v. Russell Hotel) favouring the use of red brick and terracotta, much in evidence here in Torrington Place. The building and its attached railings and gates on Gower Street are Grade II listed and described by Historic England as designed in the 'elaborate Franco-Flemish Gothic style'. Just one look at its row of gables, steep tiled roofs, oriel windows, lofty chimneys and octagonal corner turrets justifies its classification. The building also boasts wonderful rich carvings of mythical beasts, gargoyles, lion mask spouts and foliage.

Right and below: Waterstones bookshop.
(© A. McMurdo)

Waterstones bookshop. (© A. McMurdo)

During the 1950s one of the original shops in the terrace was taken over by a bookseller, Una Dillon (1903–93), who later established Dillon's University Bookshop. Una had previously worked for a mental-health charity and been involved in setting up bookstalls. In 1936, with no real experience of the bookselling industry she bought up a small bookshop in nearby Store Street. The shop, so well located beside the University of London, thrived and after the war she moved it to Torrington Place. Here, as Dillon's it became not just Bloomsbury's, but London's principle academic bookshop and by 1967 when Una retired, it extended almost along the entire block. It was really Una's resourcefulness together with her understanding of what a good bookshop should be that lead to Dillon's success. Since 1995 the bookstore has been part of the Waterstones chain. It now occupies five floors, and has a coffee shop especially popular with students called Dillons.

38. Willing House, Nos 356–364 Gray's Inn Road

Only moments away from King's Cross Station, Willing House stands out on the Gray's Inn Road due to its striking red and white façade with ornate carvings, bow windows, steeply pitched roof, and pair of winged lions guarding the main doorway. Today, the house is occupied by the budget hotel Travelodge, and it is highly probable

Above and right: Willing House, Travelodge. (© A. McMurdo)

Willing House, Travelodge. (© A. McMurdo)

that customers staying here are unaware of its original usage by a thriving advertising agency, Willing & Co. Extremely successful in the early part of the twentieth century the company was involved in a wide range of activities but was probably best known for its billboard and poster advertising. It also owned a chain of bookstands at several mainline railway stations and handled advertising for the railways and omnibuses, as well as the newspapers, newsagents and in London's streets.

In the latter years of the nineteenth century billboard advertising had become increasingly widespread and was considered a most cost-effective way to advertise products. Willing & Co concentrated on the development of this side of its business and soon established itself as a major presence in the market. House walls were a most popular location for advertising posters and billboards and many a local landowner was tempted into leasing out the exterior of a property for income rather than have the hassle of renting to tenants.

The Willing family business began life at No. 366 Gray's Inn Road. When the company acquired the adjacent site in the early 1900s it contracted Hart and Waterhouse to design Willing House to accommodate the new offices. The splendid building the architects created has since attracted Grade II listed status, due to the merit of its architectural style and design. The canted oriel window and intricate carvings above the main entrance, as well as A. Stanley Young's sculpture of the messenger god Mercury on the roof peak, make Willing House a visual treat. The building's features not only enhance the immediate area but also make it easy to identify the King's Cross Travelodge hotel.

39. BMA House, Tavistock Square

It is difficult now to imagine a time before Bloomsbury's squares existed but the land that BMA House occupies today was open field until the very late 1700s. The first buildings to be erected on this side of the square were dominated by the grand Tavistock House, designed, and quite probably lived in, by the property developer James Burton (1761–1837). The novelist Charles Dickens (1812–70) moved into the house with his large family in the 1850s, performing in amateur dramatics in the converted schoolroom, which he referred to as 'The Smallest Theatre in the World'. It was also where he wrote *Bleak House, Hard Times, Little Dorrit* and *A Tale of Two Cities*.

Tavistock House was later demolished and the land acquired by the Theosophical Society, a free-thinking and philosophical organisation, who commissioned the renowned architect Sir Edwin Lutyens (1869–1944) to design its headquarters on the site. Work began in 1911 but was not completed until the mid-1920s due to the outbreak of war. Subsequently, the Theosophists' finances dried up and the unfinished building was sold to the British Medical Association (BMA), who tasked Lutyens to complete the building for their head office. When BMA House was opened in 1925, almost a century after the founding of the BMA,

The opening of the BMA Headquarters in 1925. (© BMA)

Courtyard of the BMA Headquarters. (© Matthew Cheung Photography)

the organisation's role had grown to such an extent that it had become recognised as the voice of the country's medical profession. In 1974 the BMA took on trade union status, representing the interests of its GPs, consultants, specialists, junior doctors and other medical professional members. Not only acting for its doctors and workers the organisation continues to promote quality healthcare in the UK and abroad and keeps the government informed about doctors' opinions on medical matters.

Although a private building, passers-by can look through the main entrance to see Lutyen's original 'Wrenaissance'-style building, the courtyard and gardens. Two major features of note are the memorials for the two world wars: Lutyens' wrought-iron Gates of Remembrance and James Woodford's central courtyard fountain and memorial statues.

40. Rosewood London Hotel, No. 252 High Holborn

For seventy-five years this magnificent building functioned as the headquarters of the Pearl Assurance Company, until it was converted into a luxury hotel at the end of the 1990s. When the offices opened in 1914, the area around High Holborn was utterly transformed by the company's imposing Edwardian baroque frontage and carriageway entrance. The building was so grand, in many ways reflecting Britain as an imperial power, and demonstrated Pearl Assurance's ever-growing status.

Rosewood London Hotel. (© Rosewood London)

Designed by H. Percy Monckton (1857–1930), the interior was as luxurious as the exterior, with elaborate banking halls as well as a beautiful balustraded marble staircase. All these features contributed to the building being assigned Grade II listed status by English Heritage in 1974 and meant that when new owners took over the building they had to adhere to strict planning regulations to convert it from offices to a hotel.

Since 2013 the site has been home to the Rosewood London Hotel and has been returned to its former grandeur. Highlights of the hotel today include the Holborn Dining Room, once home to the east Banking Hall and the seven-storey marble staircase that sits beneath the great dome.

41. Senate House, Russell Square

Towering 209 feet (64 metres) over its neighbouring buildings, and almost a century old, Senate House is one of Bloomsbury's iconic structures and still stands out on the skyline. It was and is a real beacon; one of the country's very first skyscrapers, built in Portland stone and granite, and is a wonderful example of stylish modernist architecture. Charles Holden (1875–1960), its architect (celebrated for his work on the London underground), initially drew up plans

Above: Senate House. (© University of London)

Left: Crush Hall, Senate House. (© University of London)

Senate House and Torrington Square. (© University of London)

for a much larger single building to accommodate all the University of London's institutions, stretching northwards from Montague Place. However, funding issues and the onset of war meant that his designs became modified and Senate House ultimately became home to the University of London's Library, Chancellor's offices, halls and administrative departments.

In 1939 when war broke out the building was taken over by the government's propaganda machine, the Ministry of Information. A number of writers, such as John Betjeman, Graham Greene and George Orwell, spent their wartime careers in or associated with the building. Greene's *Ministry of Fear* (1943) and Orwell's *1984* (1949) novels both used Senate House in their writing, the former as the centre of an international spying network, the latter as home to the futuristic Ministry of Truth.

After the war the building reverted to its original use and became the hub of the university. Its globally renowned library, used by vast numbers then and now, contains exceptional specialist collections in the humanities and social sciences. Although it is not generally open to the public, it is possible to purchase a day pass for research purposes.

Senate House underwent a massive £55 million refurbishment in 2006 when many of its art deco rooms were returned to their original appearance. This has made the building all the more attractive to moviemakers, who have used its somewhat daunting façade and striking interiors in films such as *Batman Begins* (2005), *The Dark Knight Rises* (2012) and *The Theory of Everything* (2014). It has developed into a popular venue for events and fashion shows and also as a backdrop in many commercials.

42. Dominion Theatre, Tottenham Court Road

The Dominion Theatre, sited on Bloomsbury's south-western tip, is one of its most legendary landmarks. Thousands have filled this enormous venue since it was built in 1929, coming to see epic blockbuster films, opera, dance, variety acts, concerts, musicals and one-off live shows. It operated mainly as a cinema during its early years and was where long-running films such as *The Sound of Music* and *South Pacific* were shown in the 1950s and 1960s. Artistes such as Maurice Chevalier, Tommy Steele, Shirley MacLaine and Judy Garland all made appearances at the Dominion and in the 1980s Cliff Richard starred in *Time*, the Dave Clark musical. In recent years it has been the setting for Royal Variety Performances as well as charity events.

As with many buildings in the area, the Dominion has had an interesting and varied history. Initially home to Meux's Horse Shoe Brewery in the nineteenth century, it later became an amusement park where variety performances were staged in its 1,000-seat theatre. By 1911 it had become a cinema but in the next decade the site was demolished to make way for the Dominion Theatre.

Main foyer of the Dominion Theatre. (© Dominion Theatre)

Dominion Theatre (© A. McMurdo)

At the time it was developed it was one of London's largest theatres with three tiers and seating for more than 2,800; even when the Upper Circle was closed off in the 1950s it remained a vast auditorium, entertaining huge numbers every week.

Today its excellent sightlines make the Dominion a great favourite with theatregoers, who particularly enjoy its lavish and spacious foyer. Designed by William and Thomas Ridley Milburn in the neo-Renaissance style, the theatre still sports its 1920s light fittings and art deco plasterwork. Outside it has an impressive façade too, although when the Ben Elton musical *We Will Rock You* ran at the theatre between 2002 and 2014, this was almost completely obscured by a gigantic statue of Freddie Mercury. The theatre recently underwent major restoration that has returned it to its former grand appearance. It once again boasts plush, comfortable seating as well as the most beautifully ornate auditorium.

43. Former Daimler Car Hire Garage, No. 11 Herbrand Street

What makes this building so very special is the fact that it is one of very few examples of commercial garage architecture of the early 1930s in the Streamline Moderne style. Easily recognised by its curves, contours, geometric shapes and use

Former Daimler Hire Car Garage. (© A. McMurdo)

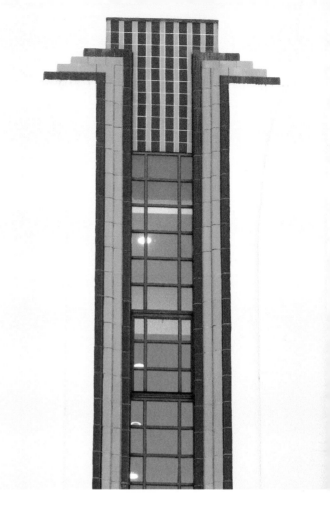

Former Daimler Hire Car
Garage. (© A. McMurdo)

of metal windows, the building is typical of the art deco movement, rejoicing in
the modern and machine age of the interwar years. It is a far cry from the earlier
art nouveau style that had promoted nature with insect wings, flowers and vine
stems. This new movement spread swiftly throughout the world following the
1925 Paris Exposition Internationale des Arts Décoratifs et Industriels Modernes,
the exciting new style being adopted for all types of buildings including garages,
hotels, cinemas, theatres and shops.

The Daimler Hire Car Garage, designed by Wallis, Gilbert and Partners, was built
as the company's head office in 1931. With offices on ground level, the garage housed
the company's fleet of de-luxe chauffeur-driven limousines on its upper floors, and
offered private car parking facilities in the basement. A spiralling ramp to the right
of the building was used to move the hire cars, used by the rich and famous, up
to the luxurious glass-fronted display showrooms on the first and second floors.
Beautifully designed with sweeping curved windows, the ramp still remains one of
the building's most iconic features. The architects of the garage were in fact much
better known for their work on the Hoover Building in West London. Constructed
around the same time, the two buildings bear great similarities in their narrow
vertical windows, chevron patterns, bright colours and white painted façades.

Daimler's association with the premises ceased in the late twentieth century when the building became a garage for taxis and coaches. It was then sensitively converted into offices for the global advertising giant McCann, which has occupied the building ever since.

Daimler Garage's architecture has always been greatly admired; so much so that an urban myth exists that Fisher Price's garage toy was inspired by this excellent art deco building.

44. The Wellcome Collection, Euston Road

This is possibly the most intimate and eclectic collection of objects connected with health and medicine you are likely to encounter. The collection was amassed by a successful American entrepreneur, Henry Wellcome (1853–1936), over many decades and demonstrates a remarkable curiosity about the human body and the world we live in. It contains over one million artifacts that range from birthing chairs, sex aids and fertility objects to bloodletting instruments, medical pharmaceutical jars, a lock of George III's hair, Charles Darwin's walking stick and even a mummified corpse. The range of objects is astounding and although only a tiny amount of them are actually on display, each one has a fascinating story to tell.

The Wellcome Collection. (© A. McMurdo)

Right: Torture chair, the Wellcome Collection. (© Science Museum, London)

Below: Tobacco resuscitator, the Wellcome Collection. (© Science Museum, London)

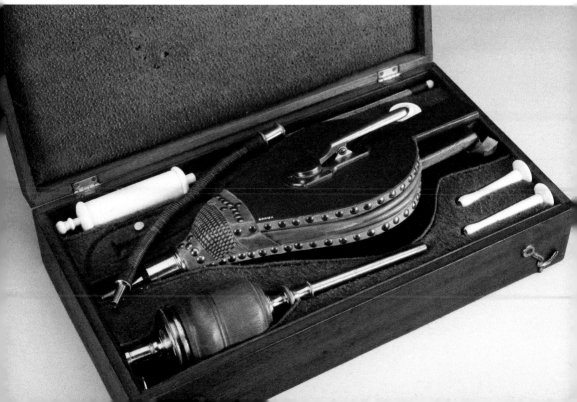

Henry Wellcome loved to travel to far-flung places collecting numerous curiosities along the way relating to history, religion, science, art and anthropology. Wellcome made his fortune in pharmaceuticals (having launched the first tablet medicine in the 1880s), and set up the Wellcome Foundation in London in 1924 to act as a research institute as well as a museum for his collection. Here he hoped that medical professionals would gather to learn more about medical science and how medicine had evolved. In 1932 he commissioned a new purpose-built headquarters in Euston Road to house his laboratories and museum. Nowadays this is the home of the Wellcome Collection with its two permanent galleries, library, exhibition and conference space, and attracts more than 700,000 visitors a year.

When Henry Wellcome died in 1936 his philanthropic vision continued with the foundation of the Wellcome Trust, which spends around $1 billion each year on global charitable research, sponsoring medical and scientific research for humans as well as animals. Some of the trust's main aims are to facilitate discussion about matters relating to environment, nutrition and welfare and to combat fatal disease, thus improving the state of health throughout the world. Wellcome remains heavily involved in UK scientific research too, providing major support to the Francis Crick Institute (UK Centre for Medical Research and Innovation) in nearby St Pancras.

45. Coram and the Foundling Museum, Brunswick Square

The Foundling Hospital is possibly one of London's most touching museums portraying the story of the city's first children's charity, today called Coram.

The charity was named after a retired British shipbuilder and seaman, Thomas Coram (1668–1751), who campaigned vigorously in the early 1700s to raise awareness of the plight of many abandoned babies and young children roaming London's streets. Having canvassed support from London's nobility and professional classes, Coram's vision for a children's hospital was finally achieved in 1739 when the king granted him a charter to set up 'A Hospital for the maintenance and Education of Exposed and Deserted Children'. At the time Britain, without any orphanages or children's hospitals, lagged behind many of its continental neighbours so Coram's Foundling Hospital was an enormous step forward.

From the start the hospital was flooded with applicants, so much so that admittance was through a ballot. Mothers had the unenviable task of drawing a coloured ball from a bag to decide their child's fate. Only white balls gained admission; black meant rejection and red, a place on the waiting list. Once admitted the children would be looked after until they were old enough to enter the workforce. Generally, boys would go into the military or become apprentices, while girls became domestic servants.

Above: The Foundling Museum Court Room. (© G. G. Archard)

Below: The Foundling Museum. (© A. McMurdo)

The Foundling Hospital's existence was greatly indebted to two men: George Frideric Handel and William Hogarth, whose art and musical works provided much needed funding. Handel's performances always attracted huge crowds and Hogarth, along with other famous artists of the day, donated works to the hospital, which in effect became the country's very first public art gallery. Sunday services in the chapel were also extremely popular with London's socialites and brought considerable private patronage to the charity.

When the hospital moved from London in 1926 the site was sold, leaving only the hospital's gateway and colonnades alongside Guilford Street. Coram's Fields, a playground strictly for children (and adults accompanying them!) was created on the site. The hospital's fascinating story is now told in the museum, which opens daily (www.foundlingmuseum.org.uk).

46. Congress House, Great Russell Street

Right in the heart of Bloomsbury is the splendid 1950s building Congress House, possibly one of the most significant modernist structures of the post-war period. It was designed to be the headquarters of the Trades Union Congress (TUC), and a lasting memorial to commemorate trade union members who lost their lives during the two world wars. David du Roi Aberdeen (1913–87) won the competition for the commission in 1946 with his bold Modernist-style plans, although work didn't start on the project for almost a decade. Amazingly, the building is fundamentally unchanged today, although recent refurbishment and modifications have updated the conference facilities and seen the building used more for commercial purposes.

David Aberdeen's innovative design centred round an interior courtyard surrounded on three sides by offices and meeting rooms. Unusually, he sited the main conference hall down a curving stairway beneath the courtyard, and gave it a roof consisting of glass hexagons, causing the courtyard, the offices and conference hall all to be flooded with natural light. The fourth side of the courtyard he filled with *Pieta*, a most poignant war memorial by the American-British sculptor and painter Jacob Epstein (1880–1959). Carved in situ from one single 10-ton block of stone, the memorial portrays a mother cradling her dead son, and is set against a dramatic backdrop of green mosaic tiles.

Passers-by can get a good view of the courtyard area from Dyott Street, looking through the glass windows into the ground-floor lobby. The free-flowing space inside is reminiscent of Le Corbusier's early 1920s designs and it is believed that Aberdeen took inspiration from his works in creating the TUC headquarters. Outside, above the portico is the impressive two-figure bronze sculpture *The Spirit of Brotherhood*. Dominating the façade, it is the work of sculptor Bernard Meadows, and depicts the strong helping the weak, so representing the very essence of the Trade Union movement. Congress House, with its Grade II* listing, is now considered to be one of London's most noteworthy mid-twentieth-century institutional buildings.

Above: Congress House. (© A. McMurdo)

Right: *The Spirit of Brotherhood*, Congress House.
(© A. McMurdo)

Pieta war memorial, Congress House. (© A. McMurdo)

47. Lumen United Reformed Church, Tavistock Place

This simple building houses a church like no other you will come across in Bloomsbury. The interior is a real architectural treat and certainly unexpected.

Seen from the street the church is a typical post-war ecclesiastical building; a geometric shape with little exterior ornamentation apart from an impressively large window added in 2007–08 when Lumen was remodelled. It is in great contrast to the original highly decorative 1827 church on the site that was celebrated for its Gothic twin towers and styled on York Minster. This earlier church was demolished following severe bomb damage in 1945 and replaced during the post-war years by the present building.

At the start of the new millennium the church authorities decided to introduce modifications to the church to make it more accessible to the local community. Local architects Theis and Khan, who carried out the project, were tasked to come up with designs that would include a new sacred space in the main body of the church, to create an inviting café visible from the street and to build an extension. Today's church appears much more welcoming than its 1960s predecessor. Looking across from Regent Square you see right into the café area, and it is not immediately obvious that the space is part of a religious building. Once inside you walk along

Lumen United Reform Church. (© A. McMurdo)

a short corridor and enter the church on the left. This is when you are unsure as to which way to look, for the architects have centred the room round an astonishing detached funnel-shaped structure, the Shaft of Light. Placed on the floor at an angle, it stretches right up to the ceiling and has an area within it for silent contemplation and reflection. This unique structure faces the brilliantly coloured Fourmaintreaux Window, which is full of vivid reds and oranges that had been a feature of the 1960s church and was moved to its present position during the redesign.

Nowadays the church has once again become a real focal point and is enjoyed by locals, the student community as well as tourists and passers-by (www.lumenurc. or.uk).

48. The Brunswick, Brunswick Square

Walking past The Brunswick I have often wondered what the original developers of Brunswick Square would make of its present-day mainly modernist style and concrete construction. The square, when it was constructed in the early 1800s, was considered a prestigious neighbourhood, home to the well-to-do and

The Brunswick. (© A. McMurdo)

professionals, with terraced town houses surrounding a central garden. Built on land that had been owned by the Foundling estate, it was situated on London's northern outskirts and was actually reputed for its good air! During the early twentieth century Brunswick Square was home to a number of the Bloomsbury Group (including Virginia Woolf, Adrian Stephen, Leonard Woolf, John Maynard Keynes, Duncan Grant and John Ruskin) as well as the author J. M. Barrie, who bequeathed the royalties of *Peter Pan* to Great Ormond Street Hospital nearby.

Proposals for the Brunswick Centre, since rebranded The Brunswick, were put forward in the late 1950s by Patrick Hodgkinson (1930–2016) and Sir Leslie Martin (1908–2000). It was to be a private, mixed-use development comprising flats, shops, a cinema and car parking. This in itself was not revolutionary, but the design of the complex was, as it aimed to provide high-density dwellings in low-rise buildings and in a style in complete contrast to the surrounding housing. The centre, when completed in 1972, was immediately controversial for its grey concrete unpainted exterior and unusual structure. To many, the massive development with its layered ziggurat terraces seemed more like stands at a football stadium than a housing and shopping complex, and did not fit in with its environment.

Some forty years on The Brunswick has mellowed into the street scene. 2007–08 saw a major refurbishment by Levitt Bernstein Architects when the façade, as

The Brunswick shopping mall.
(© A. McMurdo)

had been originally intended, was painted cream and significant improvements were made to the flats and inner concourse. In many respects it has become Bloomsbury's main high street; locals and visitors alike now flock to the Curzon, its very popular art-house cinema, as well as to its many shops, cafés, restaurants and supermarket.

49. Institute of Education (IOE), Bedford Way

This building, occupied by the Institute of Education and the Clore Institute of Advanced Legal Studies, is a wonderful example of the British modernist movement's architecture of the period. Initially designed by Sir Denys Lasdun (1914–2001) in the 1970s, it has been both highly lauded and criticised. Lasdun's brutalist architectural style and the exceptional quality of his finishes have been acclaimed by many, yet others have decried the building's colossal structure, considered to be over-large for its setting and the environment. In fact, Lasdun's design for the IOE ensured that his development corresponded in height and width with nearby Georgian terraces and was sympathetic to the urban environment.

Institute of Education. (© A. McMurdo)

Some of the building's most interesting features are its service towers that soar 115 feet (35 metres) high. Each was supposed to have a set of descending escape stairs, but only one was ever built and is in situ on the west side of the building.

The IOE is a global leading centre for teaching and research in education and social science. Former alumni include independent Nigeria's first prime minister, Sir Abubakar Tafana Balewa, and Sir Quentin Blake, illustrator, cartoonist and author.

50. UCL School of Slavonic and East European Studies (SSEES), Taviton Street

This is possibly the most unexpected building to find in a street full of Georgian terraces in the heart of Bloomsbury. Although flat-fronted and brick-built, (features in common with the adjacent houses), its apparent industrial and Eastern European appearance sets it apart from any other property in the street. One might say that it is an appropriate home for the SSEES, which runs undergraduate and postgraduate studies on Russia, Central and Eastern Europe, the Baltics and South East Europe.

Opened in 2005 the architects, Short and Associates, received much acclaim for their design, especially for its environmentally-friendly architecture. They introduced a novel system of natural ventilation, downdraught cooling, that drew down air through external chimney-stacks into a central atrium. The air was then circulated around the building, replacing the need for air-conditioning, making it the most innovative approach to energy provision at the time.

The SSEES is renowned not only for training the next cohort of regional experts but also for publishing papers and hosting conferences, lectures and briefings. Its extensive library, spread over four floors, is considered a major worldwide resource.

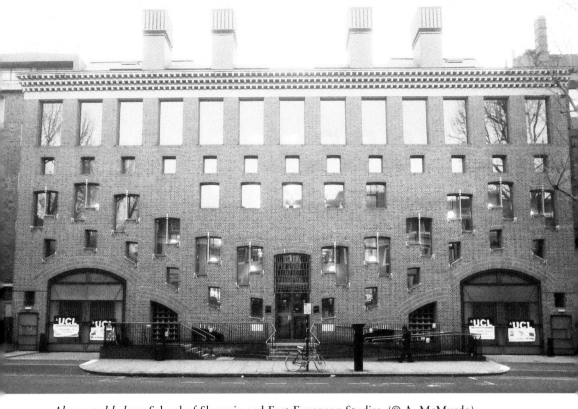

Above and below: School of Slavonic and East European Studies. (© A. McMurdo)

Acknowledgements

The author and publisher would like to thank many people and organisations that have helped in the production of this book and to acknowledge the significant part played by the author's husband, Alex McMurdo, who is responsible for the majority of images within the book. The author particularly wants to thank Jo McMurdo and Alex McMurdo for their useful comments and for proofreading the text.

Thanks are due also to the following organisations for their assistance and to those who have given their permission to use copyright material in the book: Sir John Soane's Museum, Nederlander Theatres, the TUC, the British Medical Association, the University of London, the Charles Dickens Museum, Gray's Inn, Persephone Books, the Foundling Museum, St Pancras Church, Kimpton Fitzroy Hotel, Rosewood London Hotel, Imagination, Grant Museum of Zoology, the Wellcome Foundation and Lumen United Reform Church. The author would also like to thank Amberley Publishing for commissioning this book, with particular thanks to Angeline Wilcox, Marcus Pennington and all the team for their hard work and support.

About the Author

Lucy McMurdo is a modern history graduate and native Londoner who has lived in the capital all her life. In 2003 when she qualified as a London Blue Badge tourist guide, she combined two of her major loves, history and London, and has been sharing her knowledge of the city with local and foreign visitors ever since. Always keen to explore and learn about London's secrets, she spends many hours 'walking the streets' looking out for hidden corners, unusual curiosities as well as architecturally significant buildings and ones that have a story to tell.

Lucy's tour-guiding career began over thirty years ago when she first guided overseas visitors around the UK. Since then, in addition to tour guiding she has been greatly involved in training and examining the next generation of tour guides. She has created, taught and run courses in London's University of Westminster and City University and also developed guide-training programmes for the warders and site guides at Hampton Court Palace. Most recently Lucy has been writing about the city she is so passionate about and is the author of three London guidebooks: *Explore London's Square Mile*, *Streets of London* and *London in 7 Days*.